Bird Body Parts

Clare Lewis

raintree

a Capstone company — publishers for children

Raintree is an imprint of Capstone Global Library Limited, a company incorporated in England and Wales having its registered office at 7 Pilgrim Street, London, EC4V 6LB – Registered company number: 6695582

www.raintree.co.uk
myorders@raintree.co.uk

Edited by Helen Cox Cannons and Shelly Lyons
Designed by Steve Mead
Picture research by Svetlana Zhurkin
Production by Victoria Fitzgerald
Originated by Capstone Global Library Ltd
Printed and bound in China

ISBN 978 1 406 29801 7
19 18 17 16 15
10 9 8 7 6 5 4 3 2 1

British Library Cataloguing in Publication Data
A full catalogue record for this book is available from the British Library.

Acknowledgements
We would like to thank the following for permission to reproduce photographs: Dreamstime: Mario Madrona Barrera, 12, Martin Ellis, 16, Matthewgsimpson, 22 (middle), Physi28, 22 (top), Rhallam, 17, 23; iStockphoto: John Carnemolla, 9; Shutterstock: Andreas Gradin, 8, Andrey Feodorov, cover (top middle), Bildagentur Zoonar GmbH, 7, bofotolux, 21, Chet Mitchell, 22 (bottom), Christian Musat, back cover (left), 15, 23, Cucumber Images, 18, EBFoto, 10, Eduard Kyslynskyy, 6, 23, Gallinago_media, 19, hfuchs, 11, Jack Ammit, cover (bottom), Neil Bradfield, 5, ODM Studio, back cover (right), 20, 23, Oleg Elena Tovkach, cover (top left), Philip Hunton, 13, 23, SantiPhotoSS, 4, 23, Steffen Foerster, cover (top right), Tobie Oosthuizen, 14.

We would like to thank Michael Bright for his invaluable help in the preparation of this book.

Every effort has been made to contact copyright holders of material reproduced in this book. Any omissions will be rectified in subsequent printings if notice is given to the publisher.

All the internet addresses (URLs) given in this book were valid at the time of going to press. However, due to the dynamic nature of the internet, some addresses may have changed, or sites may have changed or ceased to exist since publication. While the author and publisher regret any inconvenience this may cause readers, no responsibility for any such changes can be accepted by either the author or the publisher.

Contents

Some words are shown in bold, **like this**. You can find out what they mean by looking in the glossary.

What is a bird?

Birds have feathers and beaks. They lay eggs. They have a backbone and wings.

Robins, flamingos and parrots are birds. Penguins are birds, too.

Birds do not all look the same. Their bodies can be very different from each other.

Let's take a look at parts of their bodies.

Some birds have large eyes.

Owls' eyes help them see their **prey** at night. They need to see well at night because most owls are **nocturnal**.

Some birds, like this pheasant, have eyes on the sides of their heads. This helps them to watch out for danger all around them.

Ears and nostrils

ear hole

Most birds can hear very well.

Their ear holes are usually hidden under their feathers. It can be difficult to see the hidden ear holes.

nostrils

Birds have nostrils near the bottom of their beaks. Many birds cannot smell very well.

However, kiwis can smell well. They sniff for worms and snails hidden in the earth.

All birds have beaks.

Many birds of prey, such as this vulture, have hooked beaks. Its hooked beak is sharp, for tearing meat.

Woodpeckers have sharp, straight beaks.

They use their beaks to make holes in trees and find tasty bugs to eat.

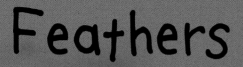

Some birds have very colourful feathers.

Male peacocks shake their beautiful tail feathers to attract a **mate**.

Sparrows have brown feathers.

Brown feathers help them to hide from **predators**.

Wings

Most birds use their two wings for flying.

This eagle uses its large wings to soar through the air. As it soars, it looks down to find animals to eat.

Some birds, such as emus, ostriches and penguins, cannot fly.

Penguins use their wings like **flippers** to help them swim through water.

Tails

Some birds' tails are useful for flying. Their tails work with their wings to help them to lift off the ground.

Tails help birds to steer through the air.

Sparrowhawks have long tails.

Long tails help sparrowhawks to change direction quickly when chasing **prey**.

Legs

All birds have two legs.

Flamingos have very long legs. They can wade through water without getting their feathers wet.

Swifts have tiny legs and feet. They can hardly walk.

Swifts spend most of their lives flying. They can fly hundreds of kilometres in one day.

Feet

Birds of prey have large claws on their feet called **talons**.

Talons are good for catching and carrying their **prey**.

duck

webbed feet

Many water birds, such as geese, swans and ducks, have webbed feet.

Water birds use their webbed feet like paddles to help them swim.

Totally amazing bird body parts!

The bee hummingbird can beat its wings 200 times per second! The wings move so fast that they are a blur!

Ostriches are the tallest birds. They can run fast but they cannot fly.

Pelicans have a special pouch under their beak. They can catch fish in their pouch.

Glossary

flipper wide, flat body part used to help animals swim

mate partner of an animal. Male animals look for female mates.

nocturnal active at night and asleep in the day

predator animal that hunts other animals for food

prey animal that is hunted by another animal

talon curved, sharp claw

Find out more

Books

Birds (Animal Classifications), Angela Royston (Raintree, 2015)

Why Do Owls and Other Birds Have Feathers? (Animal Body Coverings), Holly Beaumont (Raintree, 2015)

Websites

Learn about more amazing birds at:
animals.nationalgeographic.com/animals/birds

Find wonderful photographs and watch videos all about birds at:
www.bbc.co.uk/nature/life/Bird

Index